Story Prompts That Work

52 Detailed, Tested Story Starters for Short Stories and Flash Fiction (for Adults and Teens)

by

Carly Berg

Story Prompts that Work

Magic Lantern Press

Houston, TX

Published by Magic Lantern Press

Houston, Texas

ISBN:9780996254755

For Big Tiny

Acknowledgments

The following stories have been previously published; some in slightly different versions:

"The Shirt Off His Back" was published in *Johnny America*.

"Soul Custody" was published in *FutureCycle Flash Anthology Series*.

"Bringing Back Beulah" was published in *Devilfish Review* and in *Nazar Look: Looking Back*.

"Risen" was published in *Fiction 365* and in *Nazar Look: Looking Back*.

"Whiskey to Denim" was published in *Word Riot*.

The stories above were also published in *Coffee House Lies* by Carly Berg

Author's Note

I've heard some writers say that getting ideas isn't the problem, that they have more ideas than they could ever possibly use.

But when you write a lot of stories, especially a lot of very short stories, oh yes, you can run out of ideas. Good ones, anyway. I do. Constantly.

Whenever I went looking for writing prompts, most of what I found were things like "Write a story in which there is a kiss." "Write a story about a dog." I just didn't find much that actually gave me a good, solid start on getting a story laid out, one that I'd be excited about writing.

So, I decided to write my own book of prompts. Included are story starters from a variety of origins: reading tea leaves; take-offs on stories in the public domain (legally available for use); music; the news; fairy tales; pictures; "field trips," and so on. Different story forms are also included, in hopes of further broadening the writer's repertoire.

I figured 52 detailed prompts was at least a years' worth, but many of these prompts can be returned to again and again. My hope is this won't be a one-and-done kind of book, but one that's earned its place on the writerly book shelf, to be consulted whenever you're stuck on "where to start," well into the future.

Happy reading (and more importantly, happy writing!)

Carly Berg

Table of Contents

How to Use This Book

If you're in the mood to choose a prompt and write right now, I wouldn't dream of trying to stop you. However, if you're not quite in that mood, I advise reading this whole book ahead of time.

Story fragments have a way of working their magic in the back of our minds as we go about our daily lives. However, they need to be introduced first. After you read this, you should have all sorts of ideas swimming around in your giant, brilliant brain, getting ready for easy picking at a later date. Hey, we need to take all the freebies we can get!

Also, some of these story starters require a little advanced planning, whether that's researching board games or collecting Chinese cookie fortunes. If you get some of these easy-peasy things done whenever you're just goofing off anyway, that's less to bother with during your actual writing time.

Finally, if you don't have a notebook or habit of recording story snippets into your phone, it's time to get into that habit. When you think stories, you see things everywhere. Jot them down as they come to you. Don't let them get away!

Many of the prompts in this book are the type that can be used repeatedly. So have your notebook (or recording device) handy when you're working on a prompt from the book, too. You might come up with several story ideas for any given prompt. Save the extras for another time.

Just opening this book and picking a promising-sounding prompt is good. But when you add to that a whole system of collecting, saving, and thinking about story starters, that's even better.

Prompt #1 - A Dream

We probably all have the memories of a few dreams floating around in our minds, especially the more vivid or disturbing ones we've had at some time in our lives. I even remember a couple of dreams from as early as five or six years old. Today's prompt is to write a story based on a dream that you've had.

If you're reading ahead, keep this prompt in mind for the next time you wake up from a notable dream as well. Jot it down in your handy bedside notebook or use your phone voice recorder. As they say, chance favors the prepared mind. Get it down quick before daylight clears away the details.

Now, write your dream story.

If the resulting story seems surreal (and it probably will) that's great. People put a lot of effort into achieving that eerie, dreamscape feel and here you've pulled it off effortlessly.

Don't explain that it's a dream or show a character going to sleep or waking up. Just let it be a surreal, experimental little piece. Here's a quick dream story of mine as an example:

Chattanooga Choo Choo

People pushed in behind her and in front of her in the crowded queue. May set down the old cardboard suitcase to wipe her brow, her usually sleek hair quiff undone, bangs splayed out wildly. "What time is it? Dear Lord, I pray she gets the babies here."

Her husband, Dean, didn't answer. His gaze was fixed on the plate glass window. The hot July day outside screamed of Kool-Aid popsicles around some lucky neighbor's pool.

The eerie siren started up again from somewhere off in the distance.

"Give me the phone." May took it and pushed in numbers furiously. "Phone's dead. Goddammit. Goddammit, where are they?"

"Language, young lady," said a man behind her, causing Dean to break his trance and bristle.

"Sorry, Sir," she said to the man. "Sissy and Baby Dean!" She covered her face and wept. The snake tat showing below the sleeve of her Betty Crocker style dress flexed rhythmically as if swallowing a pinky. The line moved up.

May tapped her long red fingernails on the counter. "How many, ma'am?" the ticket clerk said. Over the intercom, a woman called: "Last train out of

Chattanooga, boarding. Last call for the last train out of Chattanooga." May tapped her fingernails on the counter. The ticket clerk said, "How many, ma'am? How many?"

Prompt #2 - People as Animals

This is one I keep coming back to just because it's just so gosh durn fun. If nothing jumps out at you right off, play with the idea for a while. Think about people you know and what animal they'd be. Do you know any human penguins, snakes, or sloths?

Without writing down people's full names (that could get you into trouble if anyone stumbled across your notes) jot down a few. Who stands out? What animal are they and why? Consider looks, mannerisms, and personality traits.

If you're reading ahead, keep this in mind as you go about your day. What kind of animal is your boss? The clerk at the grocery store? Your second best friend? Be careful because thinking this way makes you subject to bursting out laughing. (If you do, please don't explain why to the goose, frog, or pig in question).

#

Now, you've got your animal. Next, you need a situation to plop your animal person into. Pick a motivation. What do they want? Love, admiration, to go home, free bird seed?

Why can't they have what they want?

Finally, we'll need some kind of conclusion. They win or lose, or even something else.

Or, just start writing.

Don't be afraid to exaggerate an animal trait to the point that it's ludicrous.

Research the animal, if needed, but don't spend too much time on it. It's all too easy to find yourself a budding expert on the slow loris or bonobo at the end of the day, but have no story finished, or even started. Just do a quick internet search whenever you run into a specific question.

Also, do not explain. Just let the person be an animal, as if it's perfectly reasonable.

Good luck!

Prompt #3 - Unreliable Narrator

Today's prompt will be to write a story where the narrator has a mistaken grasp of the reality of the situation he's in. First, we need a situation. Here are a few examples to get you started:

Girl flirts with a casual acquaintance who she has a crush on

Child overhears parents arguing about getting divorced

Elderly person's caretaker (grown child?) abuses him and steals from him.

#

Choose one of the situations above, unless you have an idea you like better.

Now, write the story. What is it that your unreliable narrator will misunderstand?

This is often best done progressively, where the reader gets an uneasy feeling, then catches on that the situation is not how the main character perceives it. The girl believes the guy is flirting back. That encourages her to flirt more outrageously. But he's actually just being socially polite and isn't interested in her. Or, the child believes the parents are fussing over the details of a family trip to Disney Land. Or, the elderly person believes the caretaker is acting in his/her, the elderly person's, best interest.

Here's an example story of mine:

Jacob's Ride

The morning gloom lifted when Jacob saw a pretty young woman sitting alone on the bus. He passed by a couple of empty seats and slid in beside her, emboldened by the motto he'd practiced until it became second nature to him – *Always go for it.* "Good morning, he said, setting his backpack down on the floor beneath him.

"Oh. Hi." She scooted closer to the window and resumed reading her magazine, which made conversation a bit awkward.

"Are you headed to work, too?"

The girl shook her head, lipsticked mouth pursed into a pout.

He laughed, giddy from her flower perfume. "Lucky you. Oh, go on, you can get back to your magazine."

Her hair was swept up into a ballerina bun on top of her head, exposing small ears with simple diamond earrings. She pulled her black sweater close around her. Her classic style made her seem to Jacob more valuable somehow than the other girls he knew.

7

"I didn't have time to eat this morning," he said. "Care for a breakfast bar?" He took two out of his backpack and held one out to her.

She smiled and shook her head.

Nevertheless, he left one on the seat next to him.

She closed her magazine and began fiddling with her phone.

"You sure? It's only 100 calories." She might have shook her head, he wasn't sure.

"Well, I'll eat it too, if you're sure you don't want it. I'm Jacob." He held out his hand.

She smiled, touched his fingers, then let go.

"And you are?"

"Um, Isabelle."

"No kidding! I have a cousin named Isabelle. She's probably your age, too. Let's see, about twenty, twenty-two?"

"Yes. I think I'll take a little rest now." She put her purse up against the window and leaned her head against it, eyes closed."

Peaches and cream, that's what her complexion was called. He pictured her asleep with him in his double bed, her pretty head on his pillow.

The bus slowed to a stop. A few people shuffled off. Others replaced them, and the bus took off again.

He began to worry that she'd get off before he got a chance to ask for her number. "Hey, that wasn't your stop, was it?" he said.

Her eyelids fluttered. "What? Er, no. Thanks, though."

"Oh, well that's good. Isabel," he said.

He picked up the breakfast bar on the seat and tapped her thigh with it. "You sure? Last call."

He waited for a reply, didn't get one, and finally unwrapped it, a little more loudly than necessary.

"Mmmm." he said.

Out the window, he watched the scenery of trees and single family homes turn to office buildings. It was getting close to his stop. He nudged her legs with his backpack, hoping to rouse her. She moved her legs over even closer to her wall of the bus. "Oops," he said, a bit loudly. "Sorry."

The bus stopped again and the girl got up. "Excuse me," she said, looking straight ahead.

"Oh. Hey. Too bad we didn't get a chance to chat. Maybe we could grab a quick coffee sometime? No breakfast bars, I swear. Heh heh."

"Could you please move your legs?" she said.

He moved to let her pass, abashed at having been spoken to so abruptly.

The girl moved to the front of the bus but she didn't get off. She took another seat instead, just behind the driver.

Jacob figured such a polished type would want to be ready ahead of time to depart from the bus. He wondered if he should move up, too. He could apologize for offending her, then float another trial balloon. He could see himself with her, out with friends in the future, everyone laughing as he told the story of how hard to get she was.

But, shamed from the rebuke, he dithered too long and his stop approached. He fished one of his business cards out of his pocket. As he walked down the aisle, he saw that she was engrossed in digging around for something in her purse. Probably digging around for something to write her number on for him, thinking the same thing he was. She didn't look up and people were pushing him from behind. It was nearly too late. He flipped his business card and glanced back to see it land in the bun on top of her head and stick there, straight up like a price tag.

Jacob's elevated mood lingered throughout the morning. He kept checking his phone for her call.

Prompt #4 - The Afterlife

Your main character just died. (In a funny story, perhaps the people around him caused him to die of boredom).

Show your character first arriving at the afterlife. What does it look like? A waiting room, bar, nature preserve, dungeon, giant aquarium, prison?

Who's there? What do they say to this newcomer? Are they friendly, are they in cliques like in middle school, do they keep to themselves? Is there a social pecking order, or are there authorities in charge?

Do the dead look the way they did when they died, or are they older or younger? Do they keep aging?

What do they do with their time? Play board games, have jobs, interfere with life on earth?

Have your character run into someone. God, someone he owed a big apology to, a parent, the person who killed him. Perhaps an argument ensues, which leads to something worse. Which... leads to something yet even worse.

How does it end? Show how the dust settles. Maybe he reaches a new normal, or maybe he's sent back (kicked out?) to his body to live longer. (If he died of boredom as I mentioned at the beginning, maybe the people he goes back to blow off his account of his amazing adventure to the afterlife, boring as ever).

Have fun with it. When you're done, as always, go back and adjust it as needed and don't forget to try for a snazzy title.

Prompt #5 - Magical Realism

First, we'll find a real world situation and setting. Then we'll add a fantasy element to it. For this story starter, we'll just add one fantasy element to our real world situation, and it should highlight a real world condition in some way. Don't stress over that, though. Often you won't see the "message" until after you've written it. I especially enjoy writing these, so here are examples from a few stories of mine, for inspiration:

In "Empty Spots," a woman is in the midst of being left by her husband. As usual, when suffering a loss in life, she gets an actual empty spot in her body. And also as usual, she fills the empty spot with potting soil and seeds and grows strawberries from her body.

The pain of loss is represented literally, with holes in our main character's body. She tries to recover the best she can (as we all do), by filling the empty spots with something she likes (strawberries).

In "Bitten," A girl has contracted a contagious disease that turns her into a buzzing, flying creature, like a large bird or insect. She's pushed out of her family, along with her boyfriend, who contracts the same disease. They move on to live in a tree in the woods.

Her becoming literally less than human and driven away represents her feeling of being the unwanted scapegoat.

In "The Shirt off His Back," (included below) a woman's estranged husband returns, or rather his work shirt does. The shirt takes his usual spots at the table, in front of the television, and so on, then flies back out the door when it's time for him to go to work. With all the irritating parts of him gone, she finds she enjoys having him back.

#

First, choose your situation. A good place to start is with something you feel. Consider situations where you've felt strong negative emotions over something. Those are a great basis for a story problem (and hey, that way at least you get *something* out of the garbage you were put through, right?) Common painful experiences involve being unwanted, singled out for mistreatment, dumped, fired, abandoned or frightened.

You can use the situation that comes to your mind or turn it into a different situation, with different characters, but dealing with that same deep reaction.

Or, don't think it through too much and just write. Let your imagination soar and come up with a magical way of dealing with a life situation, one that's never been done before.

The Shirt off His Back

Since quitting work, I got used to doing whatever I wanted, and I didn't want to answer the door. But whoever was outside wouldn't quit ringing the bell.

I finally answered it, but nobody was there, just a shirt floating in mid-air above my porch. A long-sleeved, dark blue work shirt. The red embroidery on the pocket spelled "Douglas." My ex-husband. He said I took the shirt off his back in the divorce settlement.

"Very funny, Doug." What was he bothering me for? Granted, I'm sure his little skank closed her busy legs once she got to know him. Didn't we all. I felt around for the strings holding the shirt up but didn't find any. I searched the hedges for a blower or something. Nothing.

The shirt held out its cuff for me to shake. It raised its sleeves as if to impress me with its biceps. It clasped its cuffs together, begging.

"Oh, all right," I said. "Come in, then. But one word about the messy house and I'll get out the ironing board."

I don't usually have shirt visitors, so I forgot it didn't have a mouth or anything. I fixed two highballs, bourbon and diet Sprite, like I used to when Doug came home from work. The shirt hovered above Doug's place at the kitchen table. It rested its cuff on the drink, maybe to smooth over my gaffe. Or more likely, knowing Doug, to show off somehow.

Dinner was ready. I made friendly conversation while serving myself. "So," I said, "How's your sleazy ho?"

The shirt landed face down on the table.

"Not so good?"

It quivered all over. I couldn't tell if it cried, laughed, or pleasured itself at the mere mention of its sleazy ho. Her name was Hester. Really. Like Hester Prynne.

"Can you move?" There wasn't enough room to put down my plate of spaghetti. I felt weird not offering him any, but what would he do with it?

"Hey, guess what? I had a pool put in." I opened the vertical blinds. My Caribbean blue, built-in swimming pool sparkled, beyond the umbrella clothesline. It took up nearly the whole small yard.

The shirt's shoulders slumped.

A mean glow warmed my heart and spread through my chest. I paid for the pool out of my fat, tasty divorce proceeds. You'd think divorce would make you poorer. After all, you are dividing the assets, not multiplying them. But Doug had an inheritance, which would have been divorce-proof except that he made the mistake of mixing it in with marital accounts rather than keeping it separate. So, I got half. He deserved it. In fact, if he got smart with me, I'd march him straight out to that clothesline and hang him out to dry again.

After dinner, we moved to the living room to watch TV like we used to. I curled up in a corner of the couch. Doug's shirt hung above his recliner.

"My God. Why would anyone put a hundred grand into opening a restaurant without even working in one first? Ha, ha, the Chef Enforcer is right. Look, he's made the man cry!"

Doug's lapels tipped forward, nodding. Doug and I had talked about opening a restaurant.

The Alaska reality show was next. A family poked around in the ruins of an ancient village, picking up artifacts. The father found a stone mask.

"Wouldn't that be neat, to find something like that and hang it on your wall? Here we get so used to our regular life, we forget so much more is possible."

Doug and I had discussed tossing it all and running off somewhere exotic. He ran off with an exotic dancer instead, Hester the Molester.

Bedtime came around. It had been a lovely evening. I didn't know what to say so I just went to bed.

The shirt lurked in the bedroom doorway.

I closed my eyes, not giving it the chance to turn me down.

The shirt settled on top of me. Doug's delicious man scent carried me off to sleep and I slept through until morning for a change.

When the alarm went off, I made coffee and poured two cups before remembering. The shirt waited above Doug's customary kitchen chair.

The collar descended for my morning good-bye kiss, then Doug's shirt sailed off down the street.

Doing some chores calmed me, putting away dishes, making the bed, taking out the kitchen trash. The house would be tidy when Doug's shirt returned from work that evening. I was glad we had managed to work things out after all.

Prompt #6 - Choose a Story #1

Here's the first line: "I missed the call."

Now choose one from each category as your story starters:

<u>Setting</u>:

In a family's middle-class suburban home

In a shack way out in the middle of nowhere

1,000 years in the future

<u>Main Character</u>:

A morbidly obese woman

A henpecked husband

A pregnant teenager

Someone isn't treated well, which causes them to progressively, physically shrink.

<u>Situation</u>:

Someone sets someone's house on fire so that they can put out the fire and look like a hero to the inhabitants.

Someone believes they are destined to be a big Hollywood star.

Prompt #7 - Spiritual Child

I once had a teacher who said that every time you
interact with another person, the two of you create a
"spiritual child" together. It will be beautiful, ugly, etc.
to match the interaction between the two of you. She
paired us up and made each pair of students draw a
picture of their "spiritual child" on a big piece of brown
paper. It's always stuck in my mind.

Here's your prompt:

You (or your protagonist) run out for a half gallon of
milk. You get home and discover that the milk is
spoiled. Annoyed, you take it back to the store. The
same clerk refuses to refund your money, since
according to the date on the bottle, it's not expired. You
demand to speak to the manager. The clerk informs you
that she is the manager. She gets smart with you. You
lose your temper and slam the container down on the
counter. It bursts and milk pours out. You storm out.
On your way home, you hear a small, whiny voice in
the backseat of your car. From its words, you catch on
that it's a spiritual child created by your encounter with
the clerk. Now what?

Use the story starter above to write about a spiritual
child. Or, create your own spiritual child situation.

Here's my stab at it:

Soul Custody

When you have a connection with another person, the two of you create a "spiritual child" together. Sally knew this because she'd collected plenty of them through the years, some good and some bad. It was mostly the bad ones who showed up at her house in the flesh.

Now she tried to sleep, but the spiritual child created with her obnoxious brother, or Withbrother, as she thought of him, kicked her in the face in his sleep. Withmother woke up and took his side, as usual.

At least the sweet ones slept. Withgrandma slumbered solidly. Withjill, her best friend from grade school, cuddled up with her like a big soft doll.

Later, she awoke to banging in the kitchen. The bossy lady downstairs thumped on her ceiling with a broomstick.

Withrobert and Withleo, her spiritual brats from her two ex-fiancés, were at it again. They were wrestling in a mess they'd dumped on the floor: milk, eggs, flour, and ketchup.

By the time she got the room and boys clean, the sun was up.

She set her alarm so as not to sleep through her psychiatrist appointment, she needed more of his lovely little pills. Then she downed four shots of vodka and surrendered to blissful oblivion. Like many misunderstood souls, she required mood-altering substances to keep from losing her damn mind.

#

Doctor: As I said, it's quite an ingenious example of projection. Your mind has put your lingering feelings from these failed relationships into a personified form. In fact, I'd like to research your case further and write a paper on it.

Sally: About that prescription...

Doctor: No more medication. We need progress here, not merely symptom relief.

Sally: But, I can't---

Doctor: Whoop! Time's up.

#

The spiritual children didn't come out much in the daytime, but waited until she was in bed for the night.

Withrobert opened her apartment door and left it that way, for starters, and she did not live in a good neighborhood.

She and Robert had fought like alleycats. Their breakup was so crazy the lady downstairs set her broomstick aside and called the police.

He got the new leather sofas, she got Withrobert. She couldn't stand the little bastard, but she had to take care of him, as does any other parent with troublesome kids.

Unless... *The doctor said he wants to do research.*

Sally googled the doctor's name, and found his home address.

"Children," Sally said. "I have a surprise for some of you. The others will get something later, so no crying. Withrobert, Withleo, Withbrother, and Withmother, come on. We're going for a ride."

The bad spiritual children raced to the car. They behaved for once (sort of), not wanting to blow their chance at the mysterious treat.

She thought it best not to give the doctor a chance to say no. She sent the children to the door alone, and drove off.

#

Sally's life was now so nice she went off disability and re-joined the workforce. She quit drinking, kept her hair combed, and made new friends. The children she kept were the ones who brought her comfort and joy.

She had the doctor to thank. After all, the others were dreadful spiritual children but they were her spiritual children. Sally could not, in good conscience, have abandoned them. They had to be given to someone she trusted.

The least she could do was thank him for accepting her problem children, and ask how his research was coming along.

But he no longer worked at the clinic. Sally asked the receptionist to dial him at home.

Doctor (on the phone): You were right, they're real as hell and this is hell. They won't leave! I hope you're happy, bitch. *Click*.

Sally was happy, too pleased with her shining new life to care.

That night, after dinner and a movie with a hot date, she curled up to sleep with the sweet spiritual children.

She awoke to banging and running water.

Her bathtub overflowed, as did her bathroom and kitchen sinks. The flooding must have caused a rainstorm downstairs. The lady downstairs beat on her ceiling so hard the broomstick threatened to burst through the floor.

There was so much commotion, Sally almost missed the small figure sitting in the kitchen. "I know your secrets, bitch," Withdoctor said, writing one of them on the table with a permanent marker.

Prompt #8 - A Knock at the Door

Here's the first line: "We had just sat down to dinner when the doorbell rang."

Dinner drama is always ramped up when it occurs with company or extended family. Imagine the big traditional holiday dinner, or dinner with the boss and his wife. Who could possibly show up and turn everything upside down?

Or, depending on what calls to you, this could also start out with a routine evening supper with one person, a couple, or a nuclear family. Pass the meatloaf, and then… Who is it and what do they want?

If nothing pops out at you, try thinking of family dinners of your own or any you've heard of that went wrong, and how you could take that situation even further.

Or think of dinner scenes from movies or books. If all else fails, do an internet search for something like "dinner scenes" and see what comes up.

Alternatively, set your timer for one hour and start writing your dinner scene as fast as you can without thinking about it too much. Sometimes the conscious mind only gets in the way. If you have more than one good idea, jot the extras down in your notebook (or record them into your phone) to save for another time. "We had just sat down to dinner when the doorbell rang." Go!

This can be funny, bonkers, supernatural, sad, or who knows what else. Enjoy.

When you're finished with the first draft, feel free to change the given first line. After all, the purpose of prompts is to help you get a story down, not to hinder you.

Prompt #9 - Writing by Numbers

For today's prompt, start by numbering your paper. In my example below, I numbered my paper from zero to ten, then back down to zero again.

Then, of course, the numbering will have to be tied in with a topic to write about. I chose the old standby of love gone wrong, but the possibilities are endless.

Just a few titles off the top of my head to get you thinking: "Reasons I Hate You," "My Roommate's Crazy Grocery List," "Stupid Things My Parents/The Mean Kids at School/My Best Frenemy Did To Me," "People I Don't Like and Why," "A Dozen Ways to Get Revenge…" Well, I seem to be in a sour mood this morning!

Don't be afraid to be a little strange or funny with this one. Here's an example:

Zero

Zero is me, without you.

One is you. You are the only one. One is the number of borderlines between love and unlove where the border wars ensue.

Two is the number of imperfect paradise. Two is me and you.

Three is a crowd.

Four is the number of legs she walks on, the skunk who lured you away (with her smell, most likely).

Five is the number of times I went after her. Four phone calls and one face smack (the smack was the best).

Six is the number of times you threatened me with the cops.

Seven is the number of times I threatened you back (in my sultry mob wife voice).

Eight is the number of items I left in your car, or apartment, or through her window: one acrylic fingernail, one cheap earring, one hair clip, one receipt for two from the romantic Italian place, one phone number written on a matchbook in curly script, one lipstick smudge on your shirt, one pair of panties, and one brick (it seemed traditional).

Nine times I begged you to return.

Ten is the number of months of my (suspended) jail sentence.

Nine is the number of cats I took in (it seemed traditional).

Eight is my number of one-night stands for the month.

Seven is the number bottles of wine drunk alone this week.

Six is my number of therapy sessions.

Five suicide notes (total).

Four dates with one-night stand number five.

Three is a crowd.

Two is the number of imperfect paradise. Two is me and him.

One is his number of wives. One is the number of borderlines between love and unlove, where the border wars ensue.

Zero is me, without him.

Prompt #10 - An Obsession

This can be serious or quirky. I find this to be an enjoyable, easy to write about topic. Below are examples from a few flash stories I wrote about obsessions, but feel free to use them as prompts:

A kid is obsessed with desserts. The other kids pick on him but for it but he's so dessert-focused that he doesn't notice. He steals extra desserts from the school cafeteria, earning him the admiration of the school tough kids. But he's only interested in desserts and doesn't notice their admiration, either.

A young woman is obsessed with the color pink. Everything she owns is pink, including her poodle. Her family barges into her home to stage an intervention and clears out everything pink, showing themselves to be the unbalanced ones.

A woman is obsessed with the idea that everyone wants to steal her man.

A woman, a rather lost empty-nester, becomes obsessed with the woman next door, who is in the thick of raising kids. The main character begins watching the younger woman from her window with binoculars, then stealing things from the younger woman's home to re-create the younger woman's life in her own house.

#

There's a TV show called *My Strange Obsession,* if you want to get ideas for some off-the-wall obsessions.

The trick here, as with most stories, is to show some sense of movement as you show this obsession being played out. Things keep getting worse until it all blows up. Then, it all gets sorted out into the start of a new normal, preferably in a way that's a bit unexpected, to keep it fresh and interesting.

Especially if the story is flash fiction length (1,000 words or less), the "movement" or change in the character can just be hinted at but it should be present. And the change can be small, maybe a new realization. You'll likely do this automatically without having to worry about it. But, if your story seems dull or flat when you're finished, re-read the paragraph above to help figure out how to fix it.

Pick your protagonist and his/her obsession. Write three incidents involving the obsession, with each one being more serious, and the third one leading to a "Come to Jesus" moment. Be entertaining! Then sort out what happens after the climax, and exit gracefully. Good luck!

Prompt #11 - Words We Hate

This is a little crazy and will probably be a short one, perhaps a drabble (exactly 100 words, not counting the title), or a dribble (exactly 50 words, not counting the title). But if you want to expand it or incorporate it into a larger story, you certainly can.

Most of us have words that bug us. Writers, especially, tend to be very tuned in to language. I've seen several threads on various writers' forums where people discuss words or phrases that get on their nerves.

One thing that bugs me, personally, is when bodily function words are used to convey emotions. I tend to picture it literally, so it kinda grosses me out. For example: getting my creative juices flowing, venting, let me digest that, I can't wrap my head around it, my gut tells me, plucks at my heartstrings. Now picture those things literally happening. Yuck!

Another common annoyance is when words or phrases are mispronounced, misspelled, or otherwise mistaken. For example "deep seeded" instead of the correct term, "deep seated." "Persay" instead of the correct spelling, "per se." "Peaked" instead of "piqued."

Or the ever-changing trendy slang. "Where's the beef?" from wayyy back when and originating, I believe, from a fast food commercial. "That's copacetic," more recently, I think, but still aged now. "That's krunk" (which, I've been told, can mean the item in question is either very good or very bad). These pop up constantly, so I'm sure you'll have your own examples.

Write a list of words that get on your nerves, for any or no reason. Find at least six that go together in some way.

This list of words is your prompt.

Now, let go of all reason and write a crazy little paragraph or two, using all of the words on your list. Ready, set, go!

Once you're finished with your draft, feel free to rearrange, expand and otherwise nitpick your experimental mini-story until it's just right.

Prompt #12 - Springboards and Patterns

This prompt requires a little preparation. First, we need to find a story that we really admire, to as a springboard and/or a pattern.

A "springboard" is a starting point for original story ideas of your own. Maybe you want to address an issue in the story from another point of view or you get some other idea of your own from reading the story.

We are *not* talking about plagiarism here or anything like it. This is for "inspiration" only, which is fair game.

A "pattern" is a kind of format guide, whether you follow the published story to get an idea of how many characters to use, how many paragraphs to take to set the story up, how many scenes to have, or whatever.

Using another story for a springboard and/or pattern is a great way to get your own story started.

Think of short stories that you admire. Choose one to use as your story starter, as either a springboard, pattern, or both.

For a listing of links to free stories online, see the "For Further Reading" and "Free Online Fiction" sections at the back of the book.

Prompt #13 - Tea Leaf Reading

Here's an experimental little quickie. You will need:

* Loose tea. (The smaller tea particles inside a teabag don't work as well. I tried).

* A traditional (shallow) teacup. A coffee cup or mug with its more vertical sides doesn't work as well. If you don't have a real teacup, you can just pour your tea dregs out onto a small plate, when we get to that step.

* A pen and paper, numbered one to ten.

If you like, set the mood with candles or music. Make sure you're doing this at a time and place where you can muse without distraction.

This isn't the fortune-telling variety of tea leaf reading, although an internet search shows that to be very interesting, for those who are so inclined. If so, I recommend saving that for another time. It's way too easy to lose your writing time to unnecessary research!

We'll use our tea leaves to create the makings of a story.

#

Microwave an ounce or two of water until it boils, which should take less than a minute. Pour it into a teacup that has a pinch or two of the loose tea in it, about ¼ teaspoon. Let it sit for three minutes. Then pour out all but a tiny bit of the liquid. If you used a teacup, swirl it around. If you didn't use a teacup, pour the tea dregs out onto the small plate.

Now, look at it. What do the little tea leaf clumps look like or remind you of? On your numbered sheet of paper, quickly write down ten things that you "see" in the tea leaves. If all you see are tea leaf bits, keep looking at it until you get out of "everyday practical" mindset. Then you'll be able to do it.

Don't worry about getting too precise or technical with it. Just get your ten things written down.

Now write a story using your words. No complaining, because you came up with them yourself. Ha ha!

Word List

Here's mine, with a quick tiny story:

1) cigarette

2) spinach

3) cricket

4) paper bag

5) parasol

6) star

Carly Berg

7) hammer

8) dart

9) log

10) bug

Smoking It

The other <u>cricket </u>players told me that since the medical establishment had determined e-cigs were bad for you (which I could have told them to begin with), the new safer, healthier smoke was <u>spinach</u> <u>cigarettes</u>. They said, hey, it's a vegetable. How bad could it be?

Someone passed it to me and I took it because I needed all the cool points I could get since I carried a <u>parasol</u> above my head while I played. It was not my fault that I was fair-skinned and allergic to sunblock. Once I tried playing with a <u>paper bag</u> over my head instead, with two holes cut out for my eyes, but some guys will <u>bug</u> you no matter what you do.

So I took a toke off the <u>log</u>. It turned out to be just another trick but I didn't inhale and the joke was on them.

They all got <u>hammer</u>ed and couldn't stand up straight so I <u>dart</u>ed all over the field with my parasol held high and I was the <u>star</u> of the game.

Prompt #14 - The News

Preparation: Consider hot topics in the news. Offbeat tidbits, celebrity ridiculousness, and new scientific finds are all good bets.

Choose your news story. Either print it out, or save it on your computer.

Now, use the news story as a springboard for your own story. If you want to make your story a faux news report, use the original as a pattern as well.

If you're running short on ideas of where to go now, try one of these:

To do a parody of the original news article, look for three places to twist the original news issue, at the beginning, middle, and end.

Or, make your character respond to whatever's in front of him in an unexpected way, rather than any of the usual responses that come to you. When your character responds to whatever comes of that, twist it again. Have him respond in a way that's not expected yet again at the end, too.

Have fun with it and surprise yourself. See where you end up!

Prompt #15 - Go There

This one might take some emotional preparation and not be one you want to jump right into.

What keeps you up at night? What are your personal "issues," the ones you don't want to write stories about? Yes. Go there (assuming you're up for it, of course).

Don't worry, you'll have your main character dealing with it, not yourself. (Whew!) You can also alter the situation, type of characters and so on. It doesn't need to be recognizable.

You can go at it from an absurd angle such as having the main character act like she loves whatever the awful thing is, tell it from an opposing point of view, or write it smart-aleck style. Don't be afraid to mix it up. The idea is to hit on a universal truth about that inner feeling of being alone, misunderstood, guilty, fearful, shamed, etcetera.

Sometimes we like to stay away from the hard truths and focus on lighter or more distant stuff instead. But truth, done well, resonates.

If you don't want to stay with it too long, you can make it a drabble, a dribble, or twit-fic (twitter-length fiction, 140 characters or less including spaces, punctuation, and the title).

Don't be surprised if you feel lighter afterwards. Writing is cheap therapy!

Prompt #16 - With Words Alone

Here's a tricky challenge that we probably all run into sooner or later if we're in the habit of hunting down prompts.

Write a story in all dialogue. No "He said, she said" tags. No tags at all, in fact, and no inner thoughts. Dialogue *only*.

It's a great little exercise for realizing how much extra we tend to add. Dialogue often holds its own without the constant addition of dialogue tags or descriptions of small motions or facial expressions. It's also a chance to work on making your characters sound different from one another (as they would in real life).

Tips:

Try to stick to only two people in the conversation. Or even one person, such as one side of a telephone call.

If you use two characters, make their speech differ from each other's, as mentioned above. Write one the way you usually would. For the other, think of someone you know personally who has a pattern of speech that stands out. Maybe they tend to use short, authoritative sentences or meander on to make a point. Do they speak with an accent, use lots of clichés, frequently mispronounce words, or agree with nearly everything anyone says? Have your character speak the way that real life person would speak.

Note: When writing a character's accent, a little of it goes a long way. Don't spell everything out phonetically or in broken English, for example. The reason is that it tends to annoy the reader.

Finally, I've found this prompt works better for me if I pick a topic or interaction that's on my mind and irritates me. Of course, twisting and exaggerating from there often makes a better story.

Prompt #17 - Its Essence is Its Opposite

This one will probably be a micro-fiction (which is a sub-category of flash fiction and under about 250 words). This one starts as a happy paragraph. The main character is in a situation, possibly one of life's "big moments" and they are pleased with what's going on.

Write that paragraph from the main character's point of view. Show just a hint of the rosy glasses view built in to the character's mindset.

Then, write the paragraph a second time below that, but omit parts of it that, if you had to choose, you might say a little overly optimistic. The thrill is a bit toned down in this second re-writing of the paragraph.

Now, write the paragraph a third time below that, cutting out even more joy. The original happy paragraph is stripped to a few words, stripped to its essence. The twist is that with those happy words cut out, the situation is now looking a bit grim.

Go back and adjust as necessary.

See my example story if you need a guide to let you know what the heck I'm talking about today!

Another time, you might want to try reversing it. Start out with a complaining first paragraph and whittle it down until only something good is left. The person actually strangely likes whatever they're complaining about.

Or start out writing that spare last paragraph and progressively add words on to the next two paragraphs, with the final message being longer than the first, rather than shorter, but still containing a much different message from the first one.

#

Here's an example:

Candace

Candace heard the minister's words from afar, visions of the future swirling in her mind. Her groom, the strong silent type, grown content in her love. They'd have a cozy house, filled with babies and light.

Candace heard words in her mind. Her groom, the silent type. They'd have a cozy house, with babies.

Her groom, silent. They'd have a house, with babies.

Prompt #18 - Twisted Fairy Tale #1

The old fairy tales we all grew up with are in the public domain. That means we get to use them!

Choose one of the following fairy tales:

Cinderella

Goldilocks

Snow White

Jack and the Beanstalk

The Emperor's New Clothes

Rumpelstiltskin

The Princess and the Pea

#

Find your chosen fairy tale online and print it out. Consider ways you could shake it up. What if Goldilocks was not the innocent little girl she would have us believe, but actually a burglar? Do Cinderella's step-sisters have another side of that story for us?

Write your own version, using the printed-out story as a springboard and/or pattern.

Prompt #19 - Objects

Here's a good one for when you just can't seem to get settled in and start writing.

Go around your house and grab six objects. You can do this quickly and randomly, or give it a little thought, if you like. Ready, go!

#

What did you get? Write down the names of your six chosen items.

Use all six words on your list in your story.

If nothing comes to you right away, spend a few minutes looking at your objects. Consider getting a nice hot or cold beverage, lighting a candle, and letting your mind go with it.

My six items

Crystal ball

Giant clamshell

Book

Taco wrapper

Lipstick

Silver high heels

#

Here's my try:

Passing

Lana awoke too early. The lilting of the sea, which normally reminded her of home, pushed her nausea beyond the tolerable. She barely made it to the cabin's tiny restroom before retching.

In the mirror, her own face alarmed her. It was pale, with wild makeup smears, mouth swollen, and eyes red-rimmed. She definitely looked like something that had crawled out of the sea.

Her giant clamshell and crystal ball, souvenirs from some ports of call, were on the floor, in a jumble with a bunch of taco wrappers (she didn't eat red meat), an empty rum bottle, and a pair of men's underwear. She vaguely remembered bringing some guy back to her room, fighting with him, then luring him out onto the deck with her song. She must have been crazy drunk to let a man enter her cabin. She cringed, trying to remember how far he'd gotten. Oh well, he couldn't tell anyone.

Why oh why does it go this way. Every day, every every damn day played in her mind like a song. Perhaps it was a song. She sang lots of songs. After her paid gig singing in the lounge last night, she'd sung along with Kurt (the piano man) and the guests at the piano bar, well into the midnight hours. She wondered about Kurt, with his big suitcoat on even in the balmiest tropical nights. He came across as just formal, but he could be hiding under the oversized evening jacket, and those little things he'd said. Surely, she wasn't the only one.

Lana called room service to bring her customary kelp smoothie, then stepped into the shower. She received star treatment for a cruise ship employee because she'd been a big name all along the eastern seaboard at one time and her name still got people booked.

Too much drink nearly sunk her on land but the cruise line got the best out of her. She was something of a captive there on the ship. The lounge manager kept an eye on her in the hours before her nightly gig.

Lana spent the day idly reading fashion magazines. After a seafood dinner in her room, she fixed her hair and makeup in her usual dramatic style, tucked her fishtail up under her gown, and slipped on her silver high heels. She headed for the lounge, vowing to only drink wine.

Prompt #20 - Changes in Latitude, Changes in Attitude

I happen to be on a beachy vacation right now and have noticed once again how story fragments start popping up in my mind whenever I'm in new surroundings. However, sorry, but a vacation is not required for this prompt. Just taking your notebook and pen to a coffee shop, park, or other place outside of your usual routine will do. Any old place will do as long as it's different. New places = fresh stimuli to wake up your imagination.

#

So, now you're there. Expect to promptly freeze in place and have no ideas. If so, free write. Don't worry about forming full sentences or anything else. Just write whatever is going on around you, snippets of conversation, things you see and smell, and any related or unrelated thoughts that pass through your mind.

Once you've hung out for a while at your leisure, perhaps had a snack, and jotted down a page or so of free writing, then you'll have your story start.

For a shortcut to the above, just write down ten things that are in your environment. For this list, "things" can include, for example, a couple arguing over by the water fountain, a fat duck waddling around like he owns the place, etc. Be sure to include anything that stands out to you as different from whatever's in your usual surroundings. For example, elevator music, a pond, etc. And then, of course, write a story using all ten of your words or phrases.

A tip: If you get stuck, go surreal with it.

Prompt #21 - That's Bizarro-ish

According to *Wikipedia*, which I think we can trust for our purposes here, "Bizarro fiction is a contemporary literary genre which often uses elements of absurdism, satire, and the grotesque, along with pop-surrealism and genre fiction staples, in order to create subversive, weird, and entertaining works."

Okay, that covers a lot of ground. Our concern here isn't to worry about a big technical debate over what is or is not bizarro fiction, so I'll just say the prompt today is to write a story that's "bizarro-ish."

Start with a situation. For example:

Jon wants to try the new little French restaurant on the corner but Sarah wants pizza.

Gina and Lloyd are both going into alcohol withdrawal but they have no money. They decide to rob a liquor store. Outside the store, Lloyd wants to turn back but Gina doesn't.

Ginger simply adores Arline's tiny, expensive teacup poodle. She wants it.

#

Choose one of the above or come up with one of your
own. Start writing but take it a few steps beyond sanity
and beyond reality. Consider having the weirdness
stand for something or highlight a facet of real life in
some way.

For example, maybe Jon and Sarah get into a heated
argument. Jon thinks Sarah's too boring, uninterested in
trying new things. Sarah thinks Jon's a snob. Then each
starts snapping their fingers and with each finger snap,
a snooty French ancestor of his or a working class
Italian-American living relative of hers magically show
up. It can get more bizarre from there.

Bizarro fiction is fun to play with. Get crazy and
ridiculous beyond anything you've ever written before.
After all, it's called "bizarro."

Prompt #22 - Fish Out of Water

Today's prompt is "fish out of water." A character finds himself in a new environment that he doesn't understand or doesn't know how to navigate in some way.

A spoiled little girl is accidentally left behind after her family's adventure vacation to the rainforest. A woman from a backwoods tribe finds her.

A traditional old guy gets divorced and goes to a singles' bar in a place much larger than his small town. He enrages a small group of tough women, who find his old school ways insulting.

A proud young man from a respected family in a small, traditional village gets a job on a cruise ship, where he's ordered around like a small, not very bright child.

#

Choose one of the above story starters or come up with your own "fish out of water" situation.

Plop your character in and see what happens. Be sure to make things get worse before they get better. Let 'em have it!

Prompt #23 - **Writer's Block**

Here's an absolutely excuse-proof prompt! Save this
one for a day when your head is just full of concrete
and you can't get those words down no matter how long
you sit there staring at the computer screen.

You can't write? Okay then, write about that. Just think
about how you can't write and write *all* about that.

\#

When you're finished with that, go back and use all or
part of what you've written above to get your story for
the day done.

For example, have our narrator continue complaining
about not having anything to write about as three
increasingly astonishing things happen right in front of
him, and he is completely missing them as being
anything worth writing about.

Or just tidy up what you've written. Look for a quick
way to tie a bow at the end and exit from the piece,
letting your narrator's rant be your story for the day.

Finally, use something in your "I can't write" rant to
pull out and use as your story starter.

Here's my "I can't write" rant. I really can't believe I'm putting this in here...

#

Writer's Block (A Rough Draft)

There's just nothing to write about today, not one single thought in my head that's worthy of even the tiniest, dullest story for even the cheesiest, smallest no count free-zine. Nuth. Ing. So here I am trapped all day because it wouldn't be right to just go on and do other things when my writing isn't done. Where would that lead? I know some people who do whatever they want and, well, just look at 'em. Who wants to be that? Lazy dolts. Like animals but not as cute. But then as I said, I *can't* do my writing so I'm trapped like a rat in a trap (speaking of uncute animals).

Writer's. Block. Which of course is really writer's block head because if you didn't have a block head you'd be able to spit out something, anything, after sitting there half the day in silent misery. In quiet agony. Mute forlornness. Hushed harassment noiseless punishment still maudlinness silencio (Spanish) moroseness shushed somberness.

Now the sun's gone down and my day is gone and wasted and I'm still here looking out the window, the swimming pool looks like a pond through a pond and the bugs buzz like a buzzsaw. A cutting devise made up of insects, their tickly hairs of legs flying all over the place like splinters when sawed off. Real nice. Perhaps

I'll vomit. That would be more interesting than sitting here, purge is better than purgatory.

A dark summer night. A dark summer night and the bugs are buzzing over the old oak trees. Drusilla feels tickly hair legs by the hundreds crawling up her petticoats in unison. No, that is not a good story, it is disgusting.

There's probably nothing in my air filled head because I don't do enough that's interesting. So then why would I have anything interesting to write about. I probably need to go on a long trip somewhere far away. Far, far away. Over the rainbow, perhaps but no, clichés aren't good at all. Like a cliché, I suffer from banal boredom. Suburban vanilla whitebread isolation aloneness lonesomeness friendlessness. I should write a story called "My Trip to the Grocery Store." Or maybe "When My Husband and I Bickered over the Remote Control," except that we didn't even bicker for that long because we have three TVs. Maybe about how my shoe broke so I just got new ones at Payless, or my tooth hurt but then I flossed it and now it feels okay. Or for a real masterpiece, "It's Too Cold to Swim in the Pool Today." Or maybe is this all there is, or is it too soon for another glass of wine or it's so sad that all of our friends are crazy or oh my god I'm getting old and running out of time to live…

It was a dark summer night and the bugs are buzzing over the old oak trees. Drusilla feels tickly hair legs by the hundreds crawling up her petticoats in unison. "Eek!" squealed Drusilla, in mixed delight. Old Tom, the head stable man, walked into the barn just then and dropped his whip. And then... Oh my god where's the wine.

Prompt #24 - A Picture

They say a picture's worth a thousand words, but if a thousand words seems to be stretching it for you today, make it a drabble, at a hundred words. Or, if the spirit moves you, do five thousand words!

Think of your chosen picture as a window. You're looking out at events as they unfold.

Here's a site for drabbles that's based on picture prompts, if you want to see what others come up with: http://www.100wordstory.org

(That is, it's there at the time this book went to press. But small e-zines pop up and disappear regularly so I can't promise ya anything)

Take some time (but not too much time!) picking out your picture prompt. Play around with internet searches until you find something that grabs you. Check out the images that come with news stories, or try searches like "1800's photos," "best paintings of all time," "cats and people," or anything else that strikes your fancy. Or, pick out an old family photograph, perhaps your parents' wedding photo. Or choose an image from a print source, a magazine (*National Geographic* comes to mind), art book, or whatever you like.

Often the trick to starting a story is just getting that dang first sentence down, so here are three to choose from:

I couldn't believe my ears.

I'd never met anyone quite like _____.

"Thank you," I said, not meaning it.

#

If you're still stuck, turn on some music. It never hurts to get another one of your senses working with you on a creative effort.

Prompt #25 - A Real Character

This one might work best starting ahead of time, writing things down in your notebook (or recording into your phone) as you think of them throughout the day.

Think of someone you've known or heard of who did something over-the-top, ridiculous, or outrageous (bonus points if it was also hilarious). We all know some characters. Think of some of their usual sayings, mannerisms, and so on. Use this character for the basis of a story about "You won't believe my friend John."

The appeal of this story is that it has a feel of sharing gossip with a trusted friend. "And do you know what *else* Loony Lucy did?" can be quite delicious to read.

If thinking of a real character to use as an example isn't working for you, make up your own. Think about some "out there" things you've heard of someone doing. These things can show extremes of meanness, conceit, or buffoonery.

For example, here are just a couple of ridiculous things I've seen or heard of someone doing. (Feel free to use them, if you want):

A young guy is out driving around in his car with a few of his buddies. He says, "Let's get something to eat." He pulls in to the Pizza Inn, but keeps driving through the parking lot and stops by the dumpster out back. He jumps out of the car, climbs into the dumpster, and starts rifling through pizza boxes, looking for the "good" slices (I wonder how this one would play out on a date).

A boy feeds a long string to a gaggle of geese. The first goose greedily gobbles up the string, and soon, er, expels it. The boy takes that end, wipes it off somehow (I suppose), and offers it to the next goose. And so on, making his special "goose necklace."

#

Now, we'll need three things that our over-the-top character would do, that exhibit their extreme personality trait. If you can find three that could go together from your list, that's great. Otherwise, ad lib (if it's someone who might recognize themselves in your story, switch up places and events).

Put the three events in order from least to most outrageous.

That's the meat of your story. Tell us about your crazy main character. Don't worry if it's rough. You can always go back and neaten it up once you get the whole draft down.

When you're finished, tie that little bow at the end that wraps it up. It doesn't have to be any big deal, you just need a sentence or two that allows you a graceful exit out of the story.

You may want to have the ending tie back to the beginning in some way, perhaps going back and adding something at the beginning that goes with your ending quip, if necessary. This is always a great way to ensure your story feels complete.

Or add another aspect at the end, show Crazy Bob as a sympathetic creature in some way. The clown nose comes off for a sec at the end, adding depth to Bob.

Or… just take a clever little last jab at Crazy Bob on your way out!

Remember, we are naughtily entertaining a friend with the foibles of someone else we know here.

Prompt #26 - Technological Advances

Today's prompt is to write a story that incorporates technological advances in some major way. The story could be realistic, science fiction, humor, etc.

Here are a few prompts to choose from, or to get you started in thinking up a related idea of your own:

#

An older person is so left behind by technology that he or she can't function in the world very well anymore, or even their own home. Consider simple everyday changes as well as the big things. For example, cell phones, televisions with complicated remote controls, automatic garage doors (that sometimes get stuck), gas grills (rather than charcoal), etc. Perhaps it could be told from the point of view of a young person who thinks it's funny, and either does or does not get a glimpse at the end of how troubling it is for the older person.

#

Advances in artificial intelligence lead to people dating and trying to marry robots that look and act human. This could be told from the point of view of a partner who is threatened with being displaced by one of these, for example.

#

Or maybe instead of the robots above, the increasingly popular cosmetic surgery field has advances that allow people to have things inserted that might make them more pleasing to their partners, a chip that makes them go quiet when someone hits the "mute" button on the TV remote control, for example. Perhaps one partner pushes the other into a few of these. Then that underdog partner gets revenge.

#

Or, rather than romantic or domestic partners, this could play out between employees and an employer, or a parent and child.

Prompt #27 - Epistolary Story

For those who don't know, an "epistolary" story is one told in the form of letters, postcards, emails, texts, diary entries, etc. It's a fun departure from the usual story forms. A private glimpse into the character's life has the added kick for the reader of feeling like they're getting to snoop.

For this prompt, the letters, etc., will be from our main character only. The other party or parties can, of course, have contacted our main character as we go along but we won't include their correspondence here.

Choose the form, for example, post cards, journal entries, or emails. This may change as you go along to better fit with whatever you decide to write about. We start out just before, or just when, something happens to change things for our protagonist. Then we'll show rising tension, the big clash, and finally, reaching a tentative "new normal."

Below are two story starters to choose from, or to get you brainstorming up an idea of your own:

#

Love gone wrong is always a rich source of story ideas.

A man with a mean wife starts up a sneaky online romance. The romance builds. He may deny being married or he may talk trash about his wife. (He'd probably have sent more than five emails, and obviously would have received some in return, but his five are all we need to show for this prompt). The twist at the end is that the "other woman" is his wife, who lured him into it so she could slay him in divorce court.

Or maybe there's a twist on the twist and she regrets her treatment of him after hearing him pour his heart out to the "other woman." For a twist on the twist on the twist, he won't forgive her for tricking him, and won't stay with her.

#

Show someone having a problem with something they purchased and writing increasingly vehement letters, which then become public somehow, and get our hero in hot water. Have the product be something very personal that the buyer bought through the mail, instead of at a store, because they'd have been mortified to have anyone see them purchasing it. Something more off-beat can be fresher and funnier than the first things we may think of, so consider going with your third or fourth thought on what the product is, not your first one.

Prompt #28 - A Recycled Joke

Here's one to remind us that writing does not have to be oh-so-serious. In fact, humor sells very well so don't be afraid to get playful.

Start with an old joke, and slap the cheese out of it. Bring it to life as a real situation with real characters. There's your story starter.

Then, put a twist on it. See what you end up with.

#

For example, "A bear walks into a bar..."

After his gig in a teddy bear suit at the Build-A-Bear shop, Steven headed straight to his regular hangout, Spanky's Bar. After six hours of shrieking little girls hanging on him, he needed it. In fact, he was thinking maybe his first day on that job should be his last.

When he reached into the backseat for his clothes, he realized he'd left them at home. He considered going home to change, then shrugged, pulled the bear head covering on, and went in anyway.

The conversation lulled briefly, but none of his pals greeted him. It dawned on him that this could be fun, so he didn't greet them, either but took a seat at one of the nearby booths instead of his usual seat at the bar.

#

What might happen when Steven is around his friends but they don't know it's him, and soon forget about the costumed guy in the corner?

Here are a few more types of cheesy jokes: Yo mama jokes, Dumb blonde jokes, knock-knock jokes, why did the whatever cross the road jokes. A preacher, a plumber, and a mathematician are in a lifeboat... Remember, we're not just expanding on corny old jokes, we're personifying them into story starters.

Prompt #29 - Game Board Story

This one might take a little preparation. Also, if you intend to publish or distribute a story that's based on an identifiable board game, be aware that you'd probably be infringing on the game owner's rights. If that's your intention, when you're done you might want to change the names, rules, and so the original board game would be erased out of it. Or, if you're up for it, just contact the company and ask for permission.

Perhaps you could choose a game that's as old as the hills: checkers, chess, backgammon, dominoes, dice, or card games, for example. Now, if you own some board games, collect them and spend some time looking them over. Read the rules, think through how the game is played. Take your time, and see if any of the games jump out at you. Often if we just go through a few options, our story starter seems to choose us.

If you don't have any board games or just don't wanna track them down, look them up online and read their rules. See what "chooses you."

You can use anything about the game to mix up with your story. Or, play the game with someone (or someones) else and jot down notes as you play. Freewrite whatever comes to your mind (er, it's a good idea to get the other players' okay first. People can get crazy when repeatedly made to wait in the middle of a board game while you're writing, or when they think you're surreptitiously taking notes on their behavior!)

If you don't have the game you want to use and can't get a grip on a good story without playing it right then, consider just going out and buying it if you have a few extra bucks. You can always pass it on to some lucky kid afterwards.

The story might end up being stream-of-consciousness, with all sorts of deeper issues being spilled around the moves of the game. Or it might incorporate the game in another way:

Clue - The basis of a mini-mystery story.

Operation - For a story about surgeon ineptitude or a patient's illness.

Yahtzee- A story about gambling, or the luck of the draw in life.

Monopoly – A story about the haves and the have-nots.

…You get the idea.

Prompt #30 - Triples

This prompt is for a fun, experimental piece.

Choose a simple story situation that shows a significant turning point in the protagonist's life. For example, the main character goes on his first date since his divorce. The main character is on her way to her first day at a new school, on his way to the altar, or offered street drugs for the first time.

Write the first sentence. That's a common place to be stuck so always consider just jotting down something kind of all-purpose to get it going. You can always change it later.

For example: "Finally, someone came through the door."

What are three different ways this encounter could go, given your chosen story situation? Write your first story sentence over three different times, with empty lines in between.

Then fill it all in, having the encounter go a different way each time. These don't need to be full stories, just three different ways this simple encounter could go. Just do it, do not explain or bother with any transitions between the three little stories. Don't be afraid to get a bit crazy with it.

When you're finished, rearrange the three encounters if it makes more sense to have them in a different order. For example, if it builds in humor, make the scenes funnier as you go along. If it gets more creepy, make the scenes creepier as you go along.

Now go back and edit it, and add a suitable title. If you want to fill each of the three parts out more or add something in between the three parts or at the beginning and/or end at this point, go ahead. But don't be afraid to just let it be, if you like it the way it is.

Prompt #31 - A Song

Here's a simple but effective method I've used over and over again when I was out of story ideas.

First, you need to get into that mental space where you're in your own little world. For me, this requires either late night writing when the rest of the world is asleep, or being behind closed doors with a "Do Not Disturb" sign hanging on the door.

Second, do whatever else sets that "in the zone" mood for you. To me, it means getting my drink ready.

And, if I think of it early enough, I do my nails. I could swear I write much better when my hands are snazzy. Maybe it's mojo or maybe my eyes just stay focused on that keyboard and screen better from the visual impact of bright nail polish, who knows.

Third is my essential candle. I just gotta have a candle burning when I write, although I'd be hard pressed to explain why.

If you don't already have your writing routine down, here's a good chance to start it. You want to form a strong association over time, where you set up for your writing time and your mind gets it that it's time to get into that zone. You can just start with one thing, say lighting a candle, and add to it later.

Finally, turn on some music. I flip through for a while and try a few until I find a song that hits me just right. Then I play that same song over and over again while I write.

Music lends itself very well to daydreaming. So once you're in your relaxed writing zone, don't be surprised if a story fragment forms in your mind as you play and re-play your chosen song.

If not, go with the lyrics (google them if you're not sure what they are). The song lyrics will be your prompt. You can use the song as a whole, the title, first line, or the chorus to get you started. Whichever calls to you.

Once you're done with your story, go back and edit. Be sure not to copy any of the song lyrics if you plan to try for publication or even put it up on your own blog, because it's not legal to use them without permission. However, once you've got a draft of your story done, it's easy enough to substitute different phrases or sentences and erase the original inspiration out of it, so no worries.

Using song lyrics as prompts is one of my favorite story starters. I hope it works as well for you.

Prompt #32 - A Circular Story

In this story, there will be three short, connected sections. Something is handed over from each section to the next. And each of the three sections has a new main character. (Think of the baton that's passed during a relay race). At the end, there will be a fourth section as the thing that's passed goes back to the original main character. The thing, or that first and last character, will be changed in some way by then.

If you want to use this prompt with a longer story, each section will be longer and more complex, and/or there will be more sections. The rules are the same.

Think of a situation where something could be passed around or handed down. For example, gossip, perhaps growing more inaccurate each time it's repeated as in the old game, "telephone."

Or, say (1) Kaylee has a crush on Brandon, who (2) has a crush on Ashley, who (3) has a crush on Michael. And of course, (full circle) Michael has a crush on Kaylee. That might be fun to write, showing Kaylee's treatment of Michael mirror Brandon's treatment of her. For some reason, I'm hearing this one in my mind in a sing-songy way (sitting in a tree, k-i-s-s-i-n-g).

Or, (1) an expensive fur coat is bought by a wealthy man for his mistress, who (2) needs money and sells it to a friend of hers, who (3) decides she doesn't like it after all and sells it to a second hand store for luxury goods, where (full circle) it's bought by the wealthy man's wife. Then we see him thinking his wife knows about his affair and is flaunting the fur coat to mess with his mind.

Choose one of the prompts above or use them as springboards for a circular story idea of your own.

Prompt #33 - Fresh Clichés

In writing, we're usually told to avoid clichés like, er, the plague. But when shown rather than told, it won't be a cliché. It will be the story's message, the idea you build your story around.

Consider the following clichés. Which one calls to you the most? What story situations come to mind for it? Sometimes the first idea you have will be the least original. Keep going and see what you come up with on your second or third idea:

Out of the frying pan and into the fire.

You made your bed, now lie in it.

Pride comes before a fall.

I wouldn't touch that with a ten foot pole.

#

If none of the examples above do anything for you, do an internet search of "clichés" until you find one that does catch your interest.

If you prefer, here's a more detailed story starter:

Have your narrator do a stream-of-consciousness story, heavily laden with clichés. Rome wasn't built in a day.

Carly Berg

An apple a day keeps the doctor away. A stitch in time, saves nine. If you love something, set it free.

The narrator will be kind of freewriting, not necessarily being all that logical. Stream-of-consciousness is great for making someone seem a bit unhinged. Or, you could use a series of diary entries that get progressively more incoherent as his/her life unravels.

For deeper meaning with the clichés, expand that idea to show that this person feels like their clothing, home, relationships, job and so on are all trite, hokey, worn out, devoid of meaning. End it with a glimpse that things are turning around for the better. Or not.

Prompt #34 - Closer and Closer, Farther and Farther

Here's an experimental one. The sense of story motion (the protagonist changing in some way from the beginning to the end) is shown by them getting a different mental perspective on something or someone by literally moving closer and closer (possibly even until they view them on a cellular level).

To use an ever-popular topic, girl falls madly in love with boy. They talk, date, and grow closer. As she gets to know him better, some of the high shine wears off. Then, take that to an extreme, possibly where she even looks him over with a magnifying glass or microscope, as the story progresses and her infatuation with him ends.

So after getting closer and closer and seeing uglier proceed to ugliest, she goes in the other direction, farther and farther away. Until she's back at her original starting point but changed, in that her infatuation is over.

Or try this with something other than a love interest and/or have the person start out *not* liking the thing or person, then getting closer and closer and discovering they're actually made of stardust and beyond wonderful. In this case, perhaps the wondrous thing or person is the one who is then caused to back way off until arriving at the original starting point. The protagonist is changed at the end because he/she started out indifferent and being offered something. They are now lovesick, with that thing no longer available.

A few possible objects of desire: A love interest, a puppy, fame, being included in the "in" group, spiritual enlightenment, photographing wildlife in Yellowstone.

Here's one of mine:

Whiskey to Denim

A speck appeared past where the sand churns in the waves. Past where the whiskey-colored water turns denim.

On the waterfront, my quarter slid tight in the slot of the high-power, pole mount binoculars. The speck his ship—a speck on a speck on the Gulf of Mexico.

A crusty fisherman sailed me out to meet the ship. I paid him with jewelry: hoops, chains, rings and a fistful of gold on fire in the bright orange day, I couldn't wait.

The captain, having made me promise to give him my sandals, threw down a rope-ladder and called come aboard. He was small, so high up. I climbed, boarded. There he was at last.

There he was at last. We tango-kissed, my hair swept the deck. I took his picture with my camera. Hair two eyes one nose mouth shoulders chest stomach legs perfect prime beef.

Back home he moved in, so close I no longer recognized him in the photo, no more than when he was a speck on a speck in the Gulf. He had problems drank/gambled, they came/took away my car then scary men wanting a gambling debt for which I sold my furniture.

I had to find the source of all the troubles like the Gulf is fed by the muddy Mississippi that collects from a creek which flows from a spring. I inspected him with a magnifying glass from downstairs neighbor who's eighty and needs it to read. He thought it was funny but giant nose pores, ghastly moles flaky shin skin ground-in dirt on feet soles, gross.

Electric shut off bill unpaid spoiled food, sinking proverbial vessel. I got the microscope from soft pudgy thick glasses kid upstairs I knew he'd have one. The brat said no then yes for three cigarettes. I took scraps of his hair then nails skin mouth mucus. He was made of bugs, squiggly spidery living micro-beasts. A walking petri farm.

I watched from the widow's walk roof, for the next ship. When it sailed back out of port, past whiskey to denim, I was on it.

Carly Berg

Prompt #35 - Instructions

This prompt is a story in the form of "instructions." It can be quirky, tongue-in-cheek, smart aleck, or angry. It tells a story.

One good place to start is with something that bugs you, which you'd love to straighten someone out about. Something that isn't fair. Or, an awkward or unusual situation that you were once put into.

#

A few stories that could be written in the form of instructions:

How Not to Act When You Get Dumped

What to Say When Introduced to Your/His/Her Father

Running Your Roommate/Neighbor/Spouse Off in Ten Easy Steps

Gold Diggers' Etiquette Guide

#

If you don't happen to have any chips on your shoulder right now, then you'll have to come up with a narrator who does.

If that doesn't cause any lightbulbs to go off over your head either, just try to be funny!

You may want to collect some actual instructions from around your house or look at some online, to include in your brainstorming session. There are endless types of instructions.

#

Here are a few examples: recipes, a dog training manual, online driving directions from one place to another. An etiquette guide. A pamphlet on what to say to a grieving family, how to conduct yourself at a job interview, the directions on a box of hair dye.

Mix it up:

The recipe is for a magic spell, not dinner. What does someone want badly enough to cook up a spell over? Feel free to add more story around the recipe. Perhaps your main character is cooking up the spell when the object of it arrives unexpectedly. Or, your main character muses about the whole issue in between adding ingredients. Does the spell work?

A girl uses a dog training manual to try to make her wayward boyfriend behave.

A man follows driving directions with his wife in the car. As the ride goes along and we follow his thoughts in between bits of directions, we get the eery thought that he's looking for a place to murder her and discard the body.

#

Other times, the instructions alone are the whole story.

You could do a riff on the real instruction guides themselves. Consider self-help books. Once you settle on one, you may want to refer back to the guide itself, using it as a pattern when doing your own take on it. Consider a short parody story of, say:

How to Win Friends and Influence People

The Four Hour Work Week

I'm Okay - You're Okay

Body Language

Men are From Mars, Women are From Venus

Queen Bees and Wannabees

#

Choose one of the ideas above or just use them as a start for finding an idea of your own. If you come up with more than one, don't worry. Pick one for now and jot down the others in your notebook (or record them into your phone). You are doing that regularly anyway by now, right? Right?

Prompt #36 - Choose a Story #2

The first line for this story is: "It was a quiet morning."

Choose one of the following from each list:

Setting:

Summertime, on or near a swimming pool or natural body of water

Winter in the mountains

A small dusty desert town

Main Character:

An elderly woman

A petty criminal

A fifteen-year-old

Situation:

The main character is being held captive

The main character is out of money

The main character falls into a time warp into his/her own past or future.

Prompt #37 - Inkblot Story

Since inkblot tests are supposed to reveal something from your own mind, they're a perfect source of personalized story prompts.

Do an internet search of "inkblot tests." Briefly look over the inkblots offered, choose one, and print it out.

Then look it over and write down ten things you "see" in it. Don't over-analyze, just do it quickly.

Now, your list is your story starter. Use all of the words.

Prompt #38 - Holiday Colors

First, choose a holiday that you celebrate, and the colors associated with it. For example, Christmas brings red and green to mind. Valentine's Day is red and pink. Halloween is orange and black, Independence Day (U.S.A.) is red, white, and blue.

If you don't celebrate holidays or that idea just doesn't grab you right now, go with seasons and their colors. To me, winter would be white (snow) and brown (bare trees). Autumn is brown, yellow, and orange (turning leaves). Summer is blue (swimming pools) and yellow (the sun). Spring is green and... well I don't know what else but if you pick it, you can decide.

If you can add on a couple more colors, that's even better. White and black, if nothing else.

Second, title your story with the name of the holiday or season. You can change this later if you think of something better.

Third, list the first color and think about it with the holiday or season. Write what it could stand for in that context. Consider your memories. The narrator, of course, could be someone other than you and it could be straight narration, or contain characters. Don't be afraid to make it sad or funny.

Next, do the next color.

And so on.

When you're finished with your first draft, consider if your story would make more sense if your colors were in a different order. And if you haven't yet, see if you can weave some kind of story through them, even if it's just a change in mood as we progress through the colors. If it doesn't seem to have enough beginning, middle, and end to suit you, consider adding more story on at both ends as well as in the middle, between the color entries.

Prompt #39 - Dubious Virtues

Here are the seven heavenly virtues (plus a few extras since they're listed differently in different places):

chastity

temperance

diligence

faith

hope

charity

patience

kindness

humility

prudence

justice

courage

#

Pick one. If nothing calls to you, consider which one elicits the strongest emotional response from you. Consider someone you know who really gets under your skin due to possessing the virtue in such abundance that it's a fault, or perhaps someone who really gets under your skin because they portray themselves as being big on one of the virtues when they're not. Or, someone who you admire because of their abundance of such a trait, or the trait you most wish you had but don't…

Now, choose the character who will possess the trait: a parent, a child, a sibling, a spouse or romantic interest, a boss, an employee.

#

Finally, choose a story situation. Here are some examples to get you started:

A mother has so much hope for her useless son that it's funny, in a mean way. He's dumb, lazy and spoiled but all she can do is re-interpret his many foibles and pick on his wife.

A young man has so much prudence that his girlfriend decides at the last minute to stand him up at the altar. She looks like the bad one but in reality, she simply couldn't take any more of his plodding, boring correctness.

A charitable church woman makes her kids help get and wrap holiday gifts for underprivileged children, not seeming to realize that her own family is also underprivileged. Her children get no gifts.

An employee is so courageous in speaking out against the grievous insults to his co-workers that he's fired-

and none of his co-workers step forward to assist him or even thank him.

#

As hit on above, the character's outstanding virtue is actually a flaw in this story, either from the beginning, or later seen as a flaw because of the results it brings on.

Prompt #40 - Fortune Cookie Message

Am I the only one who just can't leave the dang things on the table? I eat lunch out often and have accumulated a makeup bag's worth of fortunes, which is a bit strange when I'm not much of a saver or collector in general. Ah well, they've come in handy a time or two.

Personally, I don't find the fortune cookie messages to be great prompts by themselves. A sentence or two with no context isn't much to go on. But I do find them fun when combined with notes on the environment they're received in.

You can easily find fortune cookie messages online. And that way, you can choose among a huge number of them so you will most likely find one that calls to you.

Use a fortune as a general prompt or as a first line, and there you go, a simple story starter.

But if you want that added story context (or just want an excuse to go get some Chinese food) consider getting your fortunes authentically. You can nab your dining companions' fortunes as well, or try to anyway.

Now, if you get takeout Chinese, pay attention to everything, from the order taker, to the food itself, to what goes on with your dining companion/s while you eat, to their reactions when you ask if you can have their fortunes. Sneak off and note or record tidbits that strike you as possible story fragments. Include any stray, unrelated, or bonkers thoughts that flit through your mind as well. (They're often the key to a wildly original piece!)

In my experience, the story ideas flow whenever you deliberately set yourself into high alert spy mode like this. In fact, I don't recall ever doing this where it didn't result in a pretty good story. It could be that the weirdness of secretly playing spy jolts my tiny brain into story mode, I really can't say. But it works for me and hopefully, for you too. Just don't tell your friends or family that you're spying on them when they're right in front of you, they may not understand. (You can easily make them unrecognizable once you're done with your story anyway, if you think that might be an issue).

If you're dining at the restaurant, great, that's even more story context. Even if you're dining alone at the restaurant, you're still on duty so pay attention to everything that goes on around you. Take in the food, the staff, décor, other people's conversations… and any stray, crazy thoughts.

#

Now, you had your dinner and you have your notes and your fortune/s. There's an excellent chance you're already writing your story by now. But if not, here are a few examples to help get you started:

#

Some of the fortune cookie messages say, "You're a winner! Present this message to your server for a complimentary dessert. *Redeemable at this visit only. No takeouts.*" The winners always seem to be dining alone, and soon make a quick trip to the restroom, never to be seen again. The restaurant owner quickly clears off the winners' tables, as if to conceal what's going on. Your protagonist has a deeper view of the restaurant's goings-on than the other staff because she's an experienced drifter, and has been living at the restaurant for free for a while now, unbeknownst to anyone.

#

Your protagonist gets hired at the Chinese restaurant and soon begins to realize all is not as it should be. Fish served on the buffet has the same distinct white, orange and black skin patterns as the koi in the decorative pond outside the restaurant door. Or there's a suspicious relationship between the manager and the owner of the pet hospital next door. Or your character thinks he's crazy when he starts wondering whether "Human beef" on the menu is really a typo after all (meant to read "Hunan" beef). (Hey, if the fortune cookie issue fades into the distance but you still get a great story, no worries!)

#

#

A sarcastic teenager is at the restaurant with his family or friends. He thinks unkind, if hilarious, thoughts about each person at the table as they read their fortunes out loud. He happens to be last, and kinda gets his comeuppance by what his own fortune says or his companions' reaction to the message he reads.

#

A couple are out at a Chinese restaurant. He reads his fortune out loud, and we are privy to his thoughts. Then it's his date/spouse's turn. She reads her fortune out loud, and we are privy to her thoughts. It becomes clear to us that they view their connection very differently. Perhaps there's a third person at the table, who has unexpected thoughts of their own behind their fortune message.

#

The last two examples above might be especially suitable for flash length stories (under 1,000 words).

Prompt #41 - Three Dribbles

Unlike poetry, prose doesn't have many form constraints. At first glance, putting form constraints on a story would seem to only make it harder rather than to give a boost to the writer. However, it is actually much easier to "fill in the blanks" than to face that sometimes overwhelming, formless blank screen.

This story will consist of three tiny, related, fifty word micro-stories.

To further start "filling in those blanks," let's toss some general topics out there:

other people's children

being fat

summertime

what goes on at work

high school

family

it was a dark and stormy night

what's behind the curtain

A kid is accepted to college. The stories are what he, his mom, and his dad think of that.

#

Choose one of the prompts above as the topic of your three related mini-stories, or go with an idea of your own. Don't worry if your dribbles, alone or together, don't seem like a traditional beginning-middle-and ending story. We'll just do what we want and call it an "experimental" story.

Prompt #42 - A New Old Story

Below are a few old stories that are now in the public domain (for those who don't know, that means they are no longer copyrighted, so you can use the characters, write remakes of them or sequels, etc. Well, of course you can *write* anything you want anyway, so I should say you can legally *publish* that writing- and that also includes posting it on your own blog).

#

Public Domain (from Dictionary.com): The status of a published work or invention upon which the copyright or patent has expired or which has not been patented or subject to copyright. It may thus be freely used by the public.

#

First, choose one of the public domain stories below.

Second, write a modern version of your chosen story.

Or, find a story that's in the public domain yourself, and use that. The *Feedbooks* website is a good source for them (at the time this book went to press):

http://www.feedbooks.com/books?category=FBFIC029000

#

"You Were Perfectly Fine" by Dorothy Parker – A young man is made aware that he proposed marriage to a girl while drunk the night before- and she enthusiastically accepts his proposal.

"Business and Ethics" by Redfield Ingalls- A young man's boss makes him an offer he can –and does- refuse.

"Bernice Bobs her Hair" by F. Scott Fitzgerald – A popular young lady coaxes her wall flower cousin into boasting that she'll get her hair cut off, as something interesting to say to the boys. Unfortunately, the cousin gets pushed socially to keep her word, with her popular cousin leading the way. But the wall flower gets brave in the end.

Prompt #43 - Freewriting

This one might seem a little unfair at first. After all, you're reading this book to get prompts, not to be told to generate them yourself.

However, the best prompts are ones that pull something out of your own mind, and stories that you have some kind of investment in are the ones most likely resonate with readers.

And this story starting method is one you can use over and over again long after you finish the last page of this book.

#

So, your assignment, should you decide to accept it, is:

Set all distractions aside.

Sit down with a timer, and pen and paper. Do not use the computer for this one! Writing with pen on paper often seems to jog the mind in a different way, for lack of a better way to put it. Don't be surprised if, when writing by hand, the writing is more personal than what you typically end up with when writing on the computer. Try it and see what you think!

Set the timer for thirty minutes. Now, write down anything and everything that goes through your mind until the timer dings. Don't worry about one thought matching the one before, punctuation, appropriateness, etc. Write about what you're doing, what you like, what you want to do, who you hate, times you'd like to live, what's in your wallet, what your cat thinks, etc.

#

After you're finished, take a short break, and then read over what you've written. How many story starters do you see? Choose the best one to use now.

Prompt #44 - Sins

The seven deadly sins are listed below, along with an associated color and animal for each.

Choose your favorite sin. Write a story in which it features prominently.

Mention the associated color and animal name somewhere in your story.

The first line of your story should be "It wasn't that bad, at first."

The last line of your story should be, "All things considered, it could have turned out worse."

See the examples below to get you started, use an idea of your own, or do an internet search on your chosen sin for yet more story ideas.

#

lust- blue, goat

Ex. A young man learns the hard way that girls are people, too.

#

gluttony- orange, pig

Ex. A morbidly obese woman encounters an angel.

#

greed- yellow, toad

Ex. A servant steals from her employer for many years.

#

sloth- light blue, snail

Ex. A slow-moving woman finally finds someone who accepts her just the way she is.

#

pride- violet, peacock

Ex. An arrogant supervisor – the kind of boss we love to hate- gets his comeuppance.

#

envy- green, snake

Ex. A new clown school graduate becomes obsessed with a peer's success.

#

wrath- red, lion

Ex. A woman finds evidence that her boyfriend is cheating on her. In the heat of the moment, she hits him upside his head with what's in her hand- the proverbial cast iron skillet. He suffers permanent, if mild, impairment from the blow. She later discovers that she had misinterpreted the "evidence" and he wasn't cheating.

Prompt #45 - Coming Home

This story can either be about someone coming home at the end of the day to a big surprise, or returning to their home town after many years away.

The first line begins: "When I arrived back home, things were different." (You can always change this later if it doesn't seem to fit quite right once you're finished).

In my story, "Now and Then," a middle-aged woman in the midst of a divorce moves back to her home town. The story is a bit sing-songy and smart-alecky about how different things (for her and in general) were in the seventies compared to now.

#

More example story situations:

A woman returns home for her father's funeral and discovers a secret. Now her father's attitude all those years makes more sense.

A man comes home after being fired from work, to find that his family members have aged ten years. The protagonist is left reeling and having to adjust to their strange new ways. The reason for it is not explained, but it's hinted that the protagonist had gotten so involved with other things that he had neglected his family and hadn't noticed the years slipping by.

A teenager from a troubled home comes home to a vision of what life will be like for her five years into the future. She steps into an apartment across the country to find her lovely, cool roommate strumming a guitar. The vision fades away and she is back in her terrible life but with a new perspective on it.

Someone seems to have moved into the basement. Our protagonist, an elderly woman, is a bit fearful but enjoys not being alone.

Choose one of the above situations or use them to help you come up with an idea of your own.

Prompt #46 - Twisted Fairy Tale #2

Choose one of the following fairy tales:

The Three Little Pigs

Red Riding Hood

Three Billy Goats Gruff

Hansel and Gretel

Rapunzel

The Ugly Duckling

The Boy Who Cried Wolf

#

Do an internet search to find a version of your chosen fairy tale that you like, and print it out.

Then go through and mix it up. What if the ugly duckling got even uglier with age? In "Hansel and Gretel," what would the witch's account of events be? Write your own version of your fairy tale, using the printed-out story as a pattern if needed.

Prompt #47 - A List Story

If you get a chance to read other people's various lists
(without them thinking you're a stalker!), it's
interesting how much you can tell about them from it.

A list story can be as short as one list. Or, it can go on
and on, as long as each additional list moves the story
forward in some way. A series of lists should start with
a list that shows us the beginning "normal," the state of
things just before everything changes, or just as
everything is changing. It progresses from there, with
tension building and the problem getting worse until it
reaches its peak in the climax. After that, it sorts itself
out into a new "normal."

#

To get started, consider looking at some lists of your
own. We have many more lists in our lives than we may
realize. A receipt is a kind of list, for example, whether
from the grocery store or for books online or a history
of on-demand movies purchased. Your monthly credit
card bill or bank statement is another list that tells a lot
about you. Your online medical record summary is
another list. What about your "to-do" list?

Another way to do a list story is by making up your
own type of list rather than using a common type as a
guide. For example: "Guys I Have Dated." "Why I Hate

Redheads." "Ways My Mother/Sister/Cat Tortures Me."

It's more story-like if there's some kind of movement as we progress down the list. For example, perhaps the narrator seems to come to a realization while writing it, reversing his original position. But if it's good anyway, or funny, clever, or insightful, that's good enough and we don't need to quibble about what form of writing it exactly is or is not.

A fairly straightforward one would be, for example, a set of progressive grocery lists showing someone obviously shopping for one person. Later grocery lists might show the food being more for two people and perhaps have things for the opposite sex included, or for a newborn, perhaps. And… what if at the end, the grocery list seems like it's for one person only again. What could you fill in, in the earlier lists, that would indicate that trouble is brewing?

Use the prompt above or brainstorm about other stories you could tell with one or more lists of various types.

When you're done, as always, edit, add a snappy title, and feel free to add more story at the beginning, middle and end, if you see any gaps.

Prompt #48 - Reality TV

The reality television shows come and go but here are a few of the topics they've covered:

Living in the Alaskan wilderness, crab fishermen, gold prospectors, huge families, bootleggers, bigamists, rich housewives, hospital emergency rooms, the morbidly obese, bounty hunting, dog and cat behavior, running a restaurant or bar, alcoholic interventions, forestry, hoarding, buying a house, travelling, psychic work, detective work, dating, prison, teenage pregnancy, building motorcycles, running a pawn shop, beauty pageants, and strange addictions.

Of course with reality shows we are getting an overly dramatic look at the different world presented. However, they can provide a fun and easy crash course in that different world (as well as an excuse to lounge around watching TV).

#

Watch a few episodes of one that interests you, if you haven't already. Take notes. Then use what you observe as inspiration for your own story.

Just remember, no copying the show characters' names, writing another episode of the show or anything else that could be perceived as using someone else's work without permission. If you see any of that in your finished story, be sure to fix it so the original show that inspired it is erased out of it.

A good place to start is with a specific story situation or story problem. Who wants what and who or what is standing in their way?

Or, make up a new reality TV show. Maybe modern day gladiators!

Prompt #49 - Choose a Story #3

The first line for this story is: "It was the kind of place that nobody stuck around in if they had anywhere better to go."

Choose one of the following from each list to start your story:

Setting:

A traveling circus or carnival

A religious cult

A hippie commune

Main Character:

A conjoined twin

A lonely teenage boy

A crazy cat lady

Situation:

The main character wants to fly

Someone is stalking the main character

People are disappearing

Prompt #50 - Your Muse

I picture my muse as quite the prima donna. Her name is Calli (short for Calliope of Greek mythology fame, of course). She's narcissistic, obviously, and not above distracting me with her spoiled demands when I'm trying to get my writing done. However, sometimes she shows up on a whim and lends her inspiration generously, so I have to put up with her.

If your muse was a person, what would he or she look and act like? How well would you get along? What are some specific incidents that might occur between you?

Write a story about you and your muse.

#

If you have a hard time getting started, here are a couple of story starters to use or get ideas from:

-People think Fred is my roommate and they tell me things like, "Why don't you get rid of that freeloader. Hey, my cousin's looking for a roommate." Unfortunately, Fred isn't my roommate, he's my muse.

-I forced myself to stay at my keyboard and type boring nonsense that I kept deleting. The sun shone brightly outside and I was pretty sure everyone else I knew was off having the time of their lives. I heard noise from the bedroom, and went in there to find Priscilla rifling through my drawers, tossing things everywhere.

"Where are those new flowery shorts?" she snapped. "I'm going to a barbecue and I want to look cute!"

Priscilla was supposed to show up at my writing desk four hours ago. They were my shorts. No, she didn't ask. And did I mention that Priscilla is my muse?

Prompt #51 - A Visit from Beyond

Your main character is surprised by someone's return from the dead. Choose from below, unless of course you have a better idea of your own!

<u>The dead person is</u>:

Their former partner

A parent

Someone they accidentally killed in a car accident

A ghost who has the wrong house

Someone famous

<u>What does the dead person want?</u>

To apologize

To have the last word

Revenge

A stiff drink

To run our protagonist's life

<u>What is the last line</u>? (Choose one of these and change it to show the appropriate gender):

"She began clearing out his side of the closet. Winter was coming. Someone could use those warm clothes."

"Do you feel better now?" she said, and faded away. It took him a long time to answer. "No," he said out loud to the empty room. 'Not really.'"

#

Other thoughts: Is there any significance to the day the dead person returned? Is it their former wedding anniversary, the traditional Sunday dinner, a year from the date of the death, happy hour?

#

Here's an example I wrote:

Risen

Drifting along would be so easy. No hour of the day or night would be different from any other, no day different from the rest. I wouldn't be sure I was alive with nothing outside myself to anchor me. I'd float around my old relic-filled house like a ghost.

So I stuck with a routine, though I didn't have much reason to. The kids weren't coming for Easter, they rarely even called. I boiled a few eggs and dyed them pink with food coloring, took a thin packet of sliced ham out of the freezer for my dinner. A small, foil wrapped chocolate rabbit waited on the kitchen table, glistening in the weak morning sun.

I put on my black hoodie and took my daily walk along the path in the woods. Today I cut back through the cemetery on a duty visit to Elmer. He rested in a garden crypt rather than the standard underground casket. I had bought it out of guilt and the funeral director's manipulation of my emotions. Elmer's burial cost more than his car.

Hello, Elmer. I plucked a stray weed from the base of his mausoleum, his tiny, ornately carved house. *The weather's finally warming up a bit.* I kept my visits with him light and surface only, like pleasant chitchat between acquaintances.

The doorknob on the little mausoleum twisted. The door creaked opened. My chest ached, as if my heart dropped into my stomach.

He emerged, stooped over, thinner and grayer than I remembered. Bruises or mold bloomed in spots on his face and hands. But, clearly, he was still Elmer.

"The weather's finally warming up a bit, is it? That crypt is so hot I thought I was in hell. Well, what are you gawking at, woman? Are you going to help me get home, or stare at me all day?"

Always with the questions, still. Questions from one who already knew everything. Too dizzy to protest, I held my elbow out for him to hold onto.

We trudged home through thick fog that wasn't really there.

"I'm hungry."

"All right, Elmer. Let me get another packet of ham out of the---"

"Get me a beer."

"I'm out of---"

"Why don't you get some, dammit?" He slammed his fist down on the table. The foil- wrapped rabbit bounced to the floor.

"Okay, I'm going." I rushed to the coat tree by the door, to put my hoodie back on.

"What else do you have to drink?"

"I have a bottle of Riesling in the cabinet, and some tequila, and --"

"Nevermind. Give me some wine first. Also, if it's not too goddamn much to ask, could I get some dinner around here?"

The day dragged on. Elmer ate, drank, and yelled at me. Then he watched TV, drank, and yelled at me. He stumbled to bed, and threw his shoe at me on the way.

My niggling doubt was answered, the one that had me waking up nights, out of breath. Elmer never said a word about missing me, or being glad to see me. He didn't ask if I was sad, here alone. He didn't show any sign of even liking me the slightest bit. He never said he was sorry.

Some people aren't going to change, no matter what kind of chance they get for a do-over. I guess that went for me, too. I served him with a smile and a splash of anti-freeze in every drink, just like last time.

Prompt #52 - Childhood

Childhood is a rich source of stories. Think of memories from your childhood. Jot down a scene that pops into your mind, as you remember it. Or write a few of them and pick the best one for now (maybe saving the others for later). There's your story starter.

#

Now, see how you can work with your scene above. Note where the child's viewpoint differs from what an adult would see. It could be that you've pretty much got a story right there, after changing the names to fictionalize it, if desired.

The ending should show some sense of movement, with the main character changed in some way, even if it's just a slight bit of growing up, from learning something new about the real adult world.

#

Examples:

A little girl viewing boys differently.

Realizing that people will die.

Catching a trusted adult doing something wrong.

That portrayal of a bit of growing up often happens naturally with stories originating from real childhood events. It lends that deeper meaning and sense of movement to the story that makes it more than just "here's what happened one time."

Or, if the story calls for it, jazz it up. Make the highs higher and the lows lower.

Scenes from childhood are freebie story starters. And of course when we get freebies, we need to take them!

Here's a (wildly exaggerated) childhood story of mine:

Bringing Back Beulah

It was the summer of Ouija boards and spell-casting and levitations that almost worked. We half-dozen little girls passed the long, hot days in the cool basement bomb shelter, scaring ourselves silly.

One Saturday, my dad came down and found us doing our thing, it was the Ouija board that time. He got really mad. He said to never, ever play with the supernatural because that was playing with fire. It was inviting the devil into your life. He said we were only allowed to do Christian things, not devil things.

My mom and dad got in a big fight about it. She said he was paranoid and repressed and we were just playing. Besides, The Church was part of The Establishment, who was invited to stick it. He said she needed to get off her neurotic campaigns and supervise the children appropriately while he worked all day.

Me and my sisters huddled together in the bomb shelter, sick over the fight, but honored to be taken so seriously. We believed our mom. Another girl had to bring her Ouija board over, because my dad threw ours in the trash. That was the summer Aunt Beulah died.

She was really Great Great Aunt Beulah, and she scared the sass out of us. Her voice was somewhere between Kentucky bourbon and peacock screech. She'd watch the fights on TV and pound her fists all the way down to the floor, screaming at the black and white screen, "Why, you son of a bitch! You dirty bastard!" The other ladies- my grandma, and aunts, and great aunts, and great great aunts- they were nice.

One of Aunt Beulah's eyes was a mashed potato. There was a big white lump, all taped over. We had to go to her house once. It was the oldest house in the world and it smelled like Vick's Vaporub. She drank "skin milk", which was the grossest thing I had ever heard of.

There was a baby crib with some horrible dolls in it and she made me and my sisters play with them. They were so old, whoever had gotten them new was probably dead. The thought thrilled us deeply, but not in a way that made us want to hold them. More like the bubonic plague, to be studied and savored from afar.

Aunt Beulah never had children. When she was young, her husband had put his head in the oven and died. I pictured it like on the Shake 'n' Bake commercial, where the lady shakes the meat in the bag of breadcrumbs first. We thought Aunt Beulah played with the horrible dolls herself; why else would she have them?

She died. The nice ladies chittered that my mom shouldn't have brought us children to the wake, but my mom always did everything my grandma didn't like. My mom took us up to see The Body, as she was then called. I'd say Aunt Beulah was the one in a crib then. She had on a long, dark dress and a rosary was twisted around her hands. Her hands and face didn't look real, but she still had her mashed potato eye.

Getting to see a real dead person was groovy. My friends couldn't wait to hear about it. I had a cold, icky feeling in my stomach at bedtime afterwards, though. My mom let me stay up late looking at *Highlights* and *National Geographics*.

Our supernatural summer progressed to séances. Aunt Beulah was the only dead person we knew, so she was our only choice of who to bring back from the dead. If we had a different choice, we would have taken it.

My older sister took my dad's lighter and lit the smiley face candle she had been allowed to buy with her allowance, after she'd promised not to light it. My younger sister said she was going to tell. Everybody else said she couldn't play, then. And besides, we'd all say she was the one who lit it. So, she took it back.

We sat in a circle, me and my sisters and three other girls, ages five to ten. My older sister said the ceremony things and then we all had to go around in a circle and say some other things, and then we chanted. *Bring*

Beulah Back. Up With Beulah. My mom had taken us to hold signs and chant something with a whole bunch of people once, so we were going with that. We had decided not to wave signs around because this was more solemn, like at church.

The smiley turned to liquid yellow with black swirls in its jar and we kept on chanting until I was lost in the rhythm of it and under a spell myself, watching the flame and chanting with the others. *Bring Beulah Back. Up With Beulah. Bring Beulah Back. Up With Beulah.*

She came back.

She swirled up from the ground, like a genie out of a bottle, in the center of our circle. Her dress was the dark one from her funeral, and she was swinging the rosary down to the floor like the boxing was on. She was not solid though, more like waxed paper, but in her real colors. Suspended up in the air, she waved like a curtain in a breeze.

The chanting stopped. The other girls fell all over each other, screaming. When I could catch my breath, I screamed too.

We bolted up the steps, stumbling over each other, and kept running until we were out in the bright, hot sunlight.

The candle was still burning. We sent my little sister in to tell on us for lighting it. My mom would go downstairs and blow it out.

My older sister and I got grounded for playing with fire. We also weren't allowed to play in the basement for the rest of the summer. Not that we wanted to; the basement was never the same secure space after that. In fact, every space was a bit less secure from then on, after coming to understand that people really do leave this world. And come back.

Authors rely on reviews to spread the word about our work. If you liked this book, a review at your point of purchase would be very much appreciated.

For Further Reading

Other Books by Carly Berg:

Writing Flash Fiction: How to Write Very Short Stories and Get Them Published (Then Re-Publish Them All Together as a Book). Magic Lantern Press, 2015.

Coffee House Lies: 100 Cups of Flash Fiction. South Coast Books, 2014.

Free Online Fiction

Below is a very brief sampling of online short fiction that you can read for free (active as of the publication of this book). Reading a wide variety of fiction is a great way to improve your own writing.

Bartleby Snopes Literary Magazine
http://www.bartlebysnopes.com

Boston Literary Magazine (flash fiction)
http://www.bostonliterarymagazine.com

Clarkesworld (science fiction and fantasy)
http://clarkesworldmagazine.com

Connotation Press: An Online Artifact
http://www.connotationpress.com

Daily Science Fiction (science fiction and fantasy)
http://dailysciencefiction.com

Feedbooks (stories in the public domain)
http://www.feedbooks.com/books?category=FBFIC029
000

Literary Orphans
http://www.literaryorphans.org

PANK
http://pankmagazine.com

Strange Horizons (speculative fiction)
http://www.strangehorizons.com

Tinhouse Blog (flash fiction)
http://www.tinhouse.com/blog/category/flash-fridays

Word Riot
http://www.wordriot.org

CPSIA information can be obtained
at www.ICGtesting.com
Printed in the USA
BVHW051145090722
641658BV00014B/59

9 780996 254755